YA
B
Put

Streissguth, Thomas,
   1958-

Vladimir Putin.

Vladimir PUTIN

Biography®

Vladimir PUTIN

Tom Streissguth

Lerner Publications Company
Minneapolis

A&E and **BIOGRAPHY** are trademarks of A&E Television Networks. All rights reserved.

Some of the people profiled in this series have also been featured in the acclaimed BIOGRAPHY® series, on A&E Network, which is available on videocassette from A&E Home Video.

This book is available in two editions:
Library binding by Lerner Publications Company,
 a division of Lerner Publishing Group
Soft cover by First Avenue Editions,
 an imprint of Lerner Publishing Group
241 First Avenue North
Minneapolis, MN 55401 U.S.A.

Website address: www.lernerbooks.com

Library of Congress Cataloging-Publication-Data

Streissguth, Thomas, 1958–
   Vladimir Putin / by Tom Streissguth.
     p.   cm. — (A&E biography)
   Includes bibliographical references and index.
   ISBN: 0–8225–2374–4 (lib. bdg. : alk. paper)
   ISBN: 0–8225–9630–X (pbk. : alk. paper)
   1. Putin, Vladimir Vladimirovich, 1952– 2. Presidents—Russia (Federation)—Biography. 3. Russia (Federation)—Politics and government—1991– I. Title. II. Series: Biography (Lerner Publications Company)
   DK510.766.P87S77 2005
   947.086'092—dc22   2004017725

Manufactured in the United States of America
1 2 3 4 5 6 – JR – 10 09 08 07 06 05

CONTENTS

As a teenager in Leningrad, Russia, Vladimir Putin practiced martial arts. He dreamed of joining the KGB, the Komitet Gosudarstvennoy Bezopasnosti (Committee for State Security) after school. In this photo, Putin, bottom, spars with a classmate in a sambo match. Sambo combines wrestling with judo.

INTRODUCTION

In 1968 a slender young man named Vladimir Putin approached KGB, the Komitet Gosudarstvennoy Bezopasnosti (Committee for State Security), headquarters in Leningrad, a city in the republic of Russia, then part of the Soviet Union. The building appeared secretive, with windows and doors tightly closed to the outside world. Here was a place of power and authority—but it was power that worked undercover. It worked at night and in disguise, using secret identities and hidden communications devices to find and punish enemies of the state. It was power that inspired fear. Everyone in the Soviet Union knew that to run afoul of the KGB was to risk life and limb.

But Vladimir Putin was not afraid. Ever since he could remember, he had wanted to be a spy. Working in this building was his dream, although a nearly impossible dream. He was just a teenager, beginning the ninth grade, and the son of a factory foreman who had fought in the Soviet army during World War II (1939–1945). His family had no friends in powerful places. He knew that rising through the ranks of the Soviet government and security services required good connections, a university degree, and membership in the government-run Communist Party—and Vladimir had none of the above.

Still, he did not turn away from his dream. He simply walked to the headquarters building and approached the first man he saw. "I want to get a job with you," Vladimir said.

The man studied the eager and deadly serious teenager. This kind of encounter was familiar to him. Many people wanted to talk to the KGB, for many different reasons. Some of them, like Vladimir Putin, were young people who wanted to be spies. The man decided not to drive this teenager away, at least not immediately. "That's terrific," he responded, "but there are several issues. First, we don't take people who come to us on their own. . . . Second, you can come to us only after the army or after some type of civilian higher education."

Vladimir was prepared for a refusal. He knew that in the Soviet Union, one didn't achieve a goal simply by eagerly asking for it. In this society, the government held power over each person's education, job, and place of residence. If a Soviet citizen asked for something, government officials could say no for a hundred different reasons, and they did not have to explain. A citizen simply had to accept their decisions or risk a lot of trouble.

But Vladimir persisted. "What kind of higher education?" he asked the man.

"Any!" came the reply.

"But what kind is preferred?"

"Law school."

The conversation soon ended, and Vladimir walked away. But just a few years later, he enrolled at the law school of Leningrad State University. This step was the beginning of a remarkable political career that would eventually bring this purposeful young man to the summit of power in a new Russia.

Vladimir Putin was born in the northwestern Russian city of Leningrad (modern-day Saint Petersburg) in 1952. Leningrad, shown above in the 1950s, was badly damaged during German bombing raids in World War II.

Chapter **ONE**

A BOYHOOD DREAM

VLADIMIR VLADIMIROVICH PUTIN WAS THE THIRD son born to Vladimir Spiridonovich Putin and Mariya Ivanovna Putin. The elder Vladimir Putin worked as a soldier and then as a factory foreman. Mariya held a variety of jobs during her lifetime, laboring in a factory, a bakery, and a laboratory, among other workplaces.

Vladimir's brothers were both born before World War II. One died shortly after birth, and the other died of diphtheria during the war. Vladimir was born seven years after the war ended, on October 7, 1952. Because his brothers had both died before his birth, he was the only child in the family. Soon after Vladimir was born, family and friends began to call him by a nickname, Volodya.

11

THE PUTINS AND WORLD WAR II

orld War II was a dark period for the people of many nations, including the Soviet Union. As soon as the war began in 1939, the elder Vladimir Putin, who had already served several years in the Soviet army, volunteered to serve again. He left behind his wife, Mariya, and their one son (the younger Vladimir Putin was not yet born, and another brother had died in infancy) in Peterhof, a suburb of Leningrad.

In the fall of 1941, German armies surrounded Leningrad. They began a siege, cutting off supplies of food and medicine to citizens. Thousands of civilians starved to death as battles raged on the city's outskirts.

To escape the German armies, Mariya Putin fled with her son into the center of the city. They lived in a sort of homeless shelter, surviving on a few ounces of bread a day. During this time, the boy died of diphtheria. Later, Mariya fell sick and unconscious, and her body was gathered up with a group of people who had already died of hunger and disease. She managed to wake up and cry out and, at the last minute, was rescued from burial alive in a mass grave.

At the same time, the elder Vladimir Putin was fighting the Germans. His first unit worked behind enemy lines, attacking German military bases and ammunition dumps. Later, while fighting near Leningrad, his group took a German soldier prisoner. Trying to escape, the prisoner flung a hand grenade at his captors. The grenade exploded, wounding Putin in both legs. He survived but walked with a limp for the rest of his life.

The Putins lived in Leningrad, a large port city in northwestern Russia in the Soviet Union. The Soviet Union, which existed from 1922 to 1991, was a Communist nation. Under the Communist form of government, the state owned all land and property and controlled every aspect of society and the economy. All stores and other businesses were run by the state. Anyone who criticized the government—whether through books, artwork, theater, or other media—risked imprisonment. Practicing religion was also forbidden in the Soviet Union. But in 1952, Volodya's mother defied the authorities and secretly had the new baby baptized, or accepted into the Christian Church.

The government assigned every worker a job and every family a place to live. In the 1950s, Volodya's father worked as a foreman at the Yegorov Train Car Factory. The family was assigned to live in a communal (shared) apartment on Baskov Lane in central Leningrad. They occupied the apartment along with several other small families.

Each family in the apartment had a room to themselves, with a shared kitchen and toilet. The accommodations were meager at best. The apartment building had no running hot water, no bathtub, and little heat. In the long and freezing Russian winters, the building was cold and damp. The Putins' apartment was on the fifth floor, with no elevator—only a stairway between levels. Rats scampered on the stairway landings and in the building's narrow courtyard.

COMMUNISM: THE IDEAL AND THE REALITY IN THE SOVIET UNION

The Communist Soviet Union was founded on the ideas of German writer Karl Marx (1818–1883) and Russian revolutionary Vladimir Lenin (1870–1924). Marx and Lenin envisioned a nation in which the state would own all land and property and control every area of the economy. Factory workers, farmers, and other laborers would all be government employees. Everyone would have a say in running government and business, everyone would share equally in the nation's riches, and everyone would work together for the good of society.

Marx and Lenin believed that Communism was an ideal economic and social system for modern, industrial nations. In a Communist state, they believed, people in all social classes and ethnic groups would be equal. There would be no kings, queens, or upper classes who ruled unjustly. There would be no wealthy business owners or landlords to mistreat or cheat factory workers and farmers.

The Communist ideal took hold in the early twentieth century in Russia, a nation that had for centuries been ruled by a czar, or emperor. In 1917, in the Russian capital of Saint Petersburg, Lenin's Bolshevik Party inspired workers and soldiers to rise up in the streets to protest hunger, poverty, and the power of the ruling classes. The Bolsheviks took over the Russian government and killed Czar Nicholas II and his family.

The Bolsheviks changed their name to the Russian Communist Party. Under Lenin's leadership, they eliminated their rivals using a secret police force known as the Cheka, which killed or imprisoned political opponents. In 1922 the Communists established the Union of Soviet Socialist Republics, or Soviet Union. Russia was the largest and most important of the nation's fifteen republics.

Led by the Bolsheviks, workers, soldiers, and sailors took over Russia's czarist government in Saint Petersburg in November 1917. Communism would soon be established as the new form of government.

The new government made its capital in Moscow, in the heartland of Russia. Saint Petersburg, the former capital, was renamed Leningrad (Lenin's City). From Moscow the government forced drastic changes on culture, society, and economic life. In keeping with Communist ideals, the government banished all private property. It seized factories and businesses, large and small. It took control of every facet of the economy.

But the Communist vision of a worker-owned and worker-controlled society quickly faded. Almost immediately, the Communist Party gathered complete control into its own hands. It outlawed all political parties except its own. People who protested against the government were severely punished.

In the mid-1920s, a leader named Joseph Stalin took control of the Communist Party and thereby the whole Soviet Union. He ruled as a dictator, a leader with absolute authority, killing and imprisoning millions of people to strengthen his grip on power. People lived in fear of Stalin and his secret police (later called the KGB). By the outbreak of World War II, in 1939, the Communist dream in the Soviet Union had turned into a nightmare.

When he was seven years old, Volodya began first grade at School 193, just a short walk from his family's apartment. All the students wore gray, military-style uniforms. At first, Volodya did not like school much. He often arrived late in the mornings. He sometimes got in trouble for fighting and playing pranks. He earned mostly Cs on his report card.

Many of his classmates joined the Pioneers, a young people's group that prepared students for membership in the Communist Party—the only political party allowed to operate in the Soviet Union. In third grade, Volodya was rejected for membership in the Pioneers

As a young boy, Vladimir joined a youth group called the Pioneers. At the age of fourteen, Russians could become members of Komsomol, above, the Communist Union of Youth, formed to teach the values of the Communist Party to young Russians.

because he wasn't a hardworking student. But by sixth grade, he had become more focused on his studies and he won acceptance into the Pioneers.

TRAINING BODY AND MIND

Volodya took a keen interest in sports, particularly those that could help him defend himself in fights with other boys. He was rather thin and short, but he had a strong determination that made up for his lack of size. When he was ten years old, he took up boxing. But after an opponent broke his nose, he immediately dropped the sport.

Then he discovered sambo, a sport that combines wrestling with the Japanese martial (fighting) art of judo. Nearly every day, Volodya walked to the Trud athletic club in Leningrad. There, instructor Anatoly Rakhlin helped him perfect his holds, throws, and defenses. Rakhlin also convinced Volodya to study judo as well as sambo.

A judo fighter uses the opponent's weight and momentum to throw him or her to the floor. Then the fighter tries to pin the opponent to the mat. Judo, like boxing, can be a dangerous sport. In training, fighters often work themselves to the point of exhaustion. But Volodya loved the mental discipline that judo demanded, as well as the sport's traditional rituals, such as politely bowing to an opponent before a match began. While still a teenager, Volodya Putin became a skilled judo fighter.

In the ninth grade, Volodya entered School 281, a high school. He studied hard, performing especially well in German class. He made rapid progress and soon became almost fluent in German. He also began to think about his future career. At first, he planned to go to the Academy of Civil Aviation, in his hometown of Leningrad, and learn to be a pilot.

Then, through books and movies, he discovered the world of espionage—spying. He learned about a thrilling secret society, where spies used code languages, tailed suspects, recruited and worked with informants, and risked their lives in strange foreign countries. One of his favorite movies was *Shchit I Mech* (The Shield and the Sword), a 1968 film about a Soviet secret agent working behind enemy lines in Germany during World War II. As an adult, Volodya looked back on his youthful fascination with spying. "What amazed me most of all was how one man's effort could achieve what whole armies could not. One spy could decide the fate of thousands of people," he explained.

Determined to become a spy, in 1968 fifteen-year-old Volodya approached the man at KGB headquarters in Leningrad. There the young student learned from the veteran agent that becoming a spy was more complicated than simply signing up. First, Volodya would have to complete university studies, and according to the KGB official, law school was the best preparation of all.

After the meeting, Volodya told his parents and judo coaches that he planned to apply to the law school at

Leningrad State University. But the adults in his life all opposed the idea. As a skilled athlete, Volodya was sure to be accepted at the Academy of Civil Aviation, they said. But getting into Leningrad University would be tough, and they worried that if Volodya weren't accepted, he'd have to join the Soviet army. They wanted him to stick with a sure thing and to study to be a pilot.

Their opinions made Volodya more determined than ever to enter law school and then join the KGB. By this time, he was earning As in almost every subject in high school. Based on his strong academic record, he won a place at the university despite very tough competition for the available openings.

WAITING PATIENTLY

Vladimir Putin worked hard at Leningrad State University, taking courses in history, literature, and languages as well as law. He spared little time for extracurricular activities, except for martial arts. During his first year at law school, he earned a black belt (master's) ranking in sambo. Two years later, he earned a black belt in judo. He remained a loyal member of the Trud athletic club, attending training camps, traveling to matches in faraway cities, and working out regularly.

Under the Soviet system, the government paid for Putin's education, but he had little money for living expenses. To get by, he lived at home with his parents. One summer, Putin worked on a construction crew,

Putin drove a Zaporozhets like the one above while he was in school at Leningrad State University.

chopping down trees and repairing houses in the countryside east of Leningrad.

His parents helped him out when they could. When his mother won a car in a state lottery (a kind of raffle), she gave it to her son. Very few students had cars, and Putin took good care of his little Russian Zaporozhets. He knew he would be in a tight spot if the car were damaged or broke down—he had no money to pay repair bills.

Four years went by as Putin worked diligently at the university. Still determined to become a spy, he remembered the time he had boldly approached KGB headquarters. He also remembered the KGB agent's words: the organization selected its agents, rather than hiring people who asked for a job. But Putin also knew that the agency kept track of promising students as they progressed through the university. He hoped the agency would take notice of him, and he waited for a call or a visit from a KGB member. But year after year, he waited in vain.

In 1975, as his graduation neared, Putin prepared himself for a career that didn't involve spying. Since the KGB hadn't approached him, he figured he'd have to work as a lawyer, the job for which he had trained.

Under the Soviet system, university officials reviewed every student in his or her final year, then placed the student in a job where the state could best use his or her skills. While Putin's review was taking place, a stranger came to the university campus to talk to him. The stranger explained that Putin would soon be invited to work for the KGB. As it turned out, the agency had been watching him all along. Although the university had planned to assign Putin to a job as a lawyer, the KGB—one of the most powerful arms of the Communist Party—took priority.

Putin felt deep relief and pride that the agency had not overlooked him. Of the roughly one hundred members of his class, he was the only one the agency recruited. He hurried down to KGB headquarters in Leningrad to fill out the many necessary forms.

KGB bosses reviewed his application and did a background check. Any trouble with the law or any questioning of the Soviet government by Putin as a university student would immediately disqualify him from the KGB. The agency found no problems, however, and Putin was accepted as a trainee. He was twenty-three years old and confident that his dream of the future was coming true: he was going to be a secret agent for the KGB.

Putin did his training at KGB headquarters, above, *in Moscow in the 1970s.*

Chapter **TWO**

THE YOUNG AGENT

THE **KGB** WAS AN ARM OF THE COMMUNIST PARTY, and party membership was required for all KGB agents. So upon joining the KGB, Vladimir Putin became a card-carrying member of the Communist Party.

In 1976, his first year with the KGB, Putin worked in different departments to learn how the agency was organized and how it operated. For five months, he worked in the counterintelligence division, whose main task was to discover and follow foreigners suspected of working as spies inside the Soviet Union. Next, the KGB sent Putin to Moscow for further training. There, he tracked dissidents—people who openly criticized the Soviet regime. He also collected information on people suspected of plotting against the

KGB History

The KGB had its roots in the Cheka, a secret police force created by Vladimir Lenin following the overthrow of the Russian czar in 1917. This force safeguarded the Bolshevik Party victory by killing or imprisoning the party's enemies—rival Communists, supporters of the czar, and others who opposed the creation of a Bolshevik-led government. The Cheka also sent agents to foreign countries to discover any plans these nations might have for toppling the new Soviet government.

Lenin's successor, Joseph Stalin, also used a secret police agency. His force was not called the Cheka but went by various other names. Intensely suspicious, Stalin had his police force arrest and execute anyone he considered the slightest threat to his power, including rivals both within and outside the Communist Party.

In 1954, after Stalin's death, the Soviet secret police agency was renamed the Komitet Gosudarstvennoy Bezopasnosti, or KGB. The KGB recruited many ordinary Soviet citizens to spy on their neighbors and coworkers, and it kept a close watch on all those considered possible enemies of the state. The KGB also ran an extensive foreign network. It used spies in many countries, including the United States, to keep tabs on threats to the Soviet Union.

state, kept close tabs on foreign visitors, and did background checks on new Communist Party members.

After his training in Moscow, Putin returned to Leningrad, where he specialized in counterintelligence and proved himself to be a capable KGB agent. He went about his work with energy and skill and earned steady promotions. The KGB was organized like a military force, with rankings for agents. Putin reached the rank of major within a few years.

He felt a strong loyalty to the KGB, but certain agency practices bothered him. For instance, the KGB routinely harassed writers and artists who spoke out against the Communist government in their works. The agency seized books and magazines that criticized the government and destroyed the work of dissident painters and sculptors. Putin believed this kind of activity accomplished nothing of value. Such persecution only led dissident groups to protest in the streets and led ordinary people who normally took no interest in art or politics to criticize the government.

Love Undercover

Still living with his parents, who by then had been awarded their own small apartment, Putin was comfortable in his bachelor life. He was young and just starting his career. It was easy for him to work and study without a wife and children to distract him. But as he grew older, he began to feel lonely. Then, in Leningrad in 1980, Vladimir met Lyudmila Shkrebneva.

Lyudmila was a twenty-three-year-old airline stewardess from the city of Kaliningrad near Moscow. She had come to Leningrad with a friend for a three-day visit. The first night, she and her friend went to see standup comedian Arkady Raikan at the Lensoviet Theater. There they met Vladimir, who had also come to the show with a friend. Vladimir impressed Lyudmila by offering to get them tickets to any show she wanted to see in Leningrad. She took him up on the offer, and they went out the next two nights. They met again a few weeks later and several times during the next few months, every time she had a few days off.

Their courtship lasted three and a half years. Because his job was secret, Vladimir told Lyudmila that he worked for the police department. As they grew closer, however, he revealed that he was a KGB agent. In 1983 Vladimir proposed to Lyudmila, and they were married three months later. The wedding took place at a restaurant located inside a riverboat, tied up along the docks on the Neva River. Afterward, Lyudmila moved in with Vladimir and his parents. Lyudmila enrolled at Leningrad State University, where she studied Spanish and French.

MORE TRAINING

In 1984 the KGB sent thirty-one-year-old Putin back to Moscow. There he trained for a year at the Andropov Red Banner Institute, a school for foreign agents (agents who were being sent abroad). Even during training, KGB agents had to keep their identities secret from one another. So they used fake names. At Red Banner, the other students knew Putin only as "Mr. Platov."

Putin's wife stayed in Leningrad while he trained, but she visited him in Moscow every month. While he was in training, she continued her university studies. She also discovered that she was pregnant.

Putin was pleased about becoming a father and pleased to be training as a foreign agent. The job meant he could enjoy the privilege of travel abroad, which was denied to most ordinary Soviet citizens. He also knew that he and his growing family would probably enjoy better living conditions in a foreign country than they had in the Soviet Union.

Putin passed the long training and final examination in Moscow. Because he spoke fluent German, the agency assigned him to Germany and gave him a choice—East or West. Germany had been divided into a democratic West Germany and a Communist East Germany after World War II. West Germany was an enemy of the Soviet Union. So if Putin chose to work there, he would have to go undercover. That is, he would have to work in secret and in disguise, so that no one would know he was an agent of the Soviet Union. To operate in West Germany, he would also have to take further training in Moscow before leaving.

East Germany, on the other hand, was an ally of the Soviet Union. The Soviets maintained a team of KGB agents in Dresden and other East German cities. These agents worked closely with the Stasi, or East German state police. If Putin decided to work in East Germany, he could start his assignment right away.

THE COLD WAR

fter World War II, the Soviet Union and the United States opposed each other in a political conflict called the Cold War. It was a war marked by distrust and hostility between the two powerful nations, but it involved little actual warfare. The Cold War pitted the U.S. ideals of capitalism (private business) and democracy against the Soviet ideals of Communism, with tight government control of society and the economy.

Many other nations allied themselves with one of the two "superpowers"—either the Soviet Union or the United States. For instance, the Soviet Union installed Communist governments in most nations of Eastern Europe after World War II. These nations were called Soviet satellites, meaning their leaders took orders from the Soviet Union. Most Western European countries had capitalist economies and democratic governments, and they allied themselves with the United States.

Germany, where Vladimir Putin worked for a time as a KGB agent, was split into Communist East Germany and capitalist West Germany. The United States and the Soviet Union each sent large armies to East and West Germany to protect against a possible attack by the other superpower.

Although the Soviet Union and the United States never directly fought one another during the Cold War, they did back opposing armies when Communists fought non-Communists. For instance, during the Korean War (1950–1953) and the Vietnam War (1957–1975), the United States sent troops and weapons to help the non-Communist armies. The Soviet Union did not send troops, but it did supply weapons to the Communists.

Putin was eager to begin his foreign work, so he chose the assignment in Dresden, East Germany.

WINDS OF CHANGE

Putin's job with the KGB was secure, as the Soviet government never stopped putting its spies and other agents to work. But the nation that had created the KGB was going through hard times and difficult changes in the 1980s. The Soviet economy was failing, and millions of people were going hungry.

In the nearly seven decades since the Russian Revolution of 1917, Communism had made little progress in improving living conditions in the Soviet Union. Nearly every family in the nation faced a daily struggle to obtain food, clothing, and other basic goods. Soviet factories could not produce enough goods to stock the shelves of state-run clothing shops, grocery stores, and bakeries. When goods were finally delivered, long lines formed. People had to wait for hours, sometimes even days, to buy what they needed. To buy a car, ordinary Soviets had to put their names on waiting lists. To get an apartment, the wait could last ten years or more.

A new leader, Mikhail Gorbachev, became head of the Soviet Communist Party in 1985. Gorbachev brought hope for improvement. He was an energetic, forward-thinking leader. Soon after coming to power, he announced important changes to the Soviet system. He began a new economic policy called perestroika, meaning "restructuring."

As part of this policy, Gorbachev allowed Soviet citizens to open small, private businesses. Their owners could run these shops without government planners telling them what to sell and how much to charge. The new policy inspired Soviet citizens to open shoe stores, flower shops, taxicab companies, and construction companies. A few private banks opened as well. In the past, such private enterprises had been against the law.

The same year Gorbachev took power, Lyudmila Putin gave birth to a daughter, Masha. The following year, the Putins moved to the East German city of Dresden. By then Lyudmilla was pregnant again. The young family moved into a government apartment, located in a complex where Putin also had his office. The Putins' next child, another daughter, was born in 1986. They named her Katya.

Putin holds his newborn daughter Masha in 1985.

Living in a foreign country was not easy or glamorous. The Putins often felt homesick in this foreign land, where the customs and language were very different from their own. But they still enjoyed evenings out at concerts, restaurants, and the theater. The KGB gave Putin a car as part of his job, and on weekends the family would tour the countryside around Dresden.

Through newspapers and television broadcasts from the Soviet Union, Putin heard about Mikhail Gorbachev's economic reforms and about another new policy called glasnost, or "openness." With glasnost, Gorbachev gave Soviet citizens more freedom to speak out and criticize government policy. After decades of being silenced, Soviet writers were finally free to express their opinions about politics and government. Such writings could have landed their authors in jail or at least under KGB surveillance (watch), in the past.

Putin supported Gorbachev's economic and political reforms. He believed that the Soviet Union needed a more democratic system of government, such as the kind found in Western Europe and the United States. In a democracy, ordinary people could vote for their leaders and participate in government. But Putin also believed in the Soviet Union and the Communist Party. In his opinion, the Soviet people needed and admired strong leaders, with power concentrated in the hands of a small group. The KGB had taught him to respect obedience, order, and clear lines of authority.

German guards patrol the west side of the Berlin Wall in the late 1980s. In 1961 the wall was built to keep East Berliners from fleeing their Communist society to the freedom of West Berlin.

Chapter **THREE**

WALLS
CRUMBLE

WHILE THE SOVIET UNION EXPERIMENTED WITH glasnost and perestroika in the late 1980s, East Germany remained a rigid, repressive state. Communist leaders held complete control over the government and allowed citizens very little freedom. East German people were forbidden to speak out against the state. They were not free to work where they liked, choose their own universities, or travel outside the country. They could not form new political parties or elect their own leaders. The Communist Party controlled all aspects of government and society.

As KGB agents in East Germany, Vladimir Putin and his colleagues kept files on people and organizations suspected of opposing the East German government.

The agents secretly took photographs of people meeting in streets, restaurants, theaters, museums, and parks. They also recruited informants to watch their neighbors and coworkers and to report on suspicious behavior. Putin's fluent command of German allowed him to speak easily with ordinary citizens and convince many of them to cooperate with the KGB. Once the agents had gathered their information, they wrote reports on their findings and sent them back to KGB headquarters in Moscow.

SILENCE FROM MOSCOW

Putin worked hard in East Germany, earning several promotions and reaching the rank of lieutenant colonel. In the meantime, the Soviet economy was falling into chaos. Despite Mikhail Gorbachev's attempts to reform the system, Soviet factories were failing, throwing thousands of people out of work. Lines for food and other basic goods grew even longer. People began to protest. They demanded more freedoms, like those enjoyed by people in the United States and Western Europe. They spoke out against the Communist system, which they blamed for their troubles.

The economic crisis—and the protests—soon spread to East Germany and the other Soviet-allied nations of Eastern Europe. Like the Soviets, the East Germans took their protests to the streets. In November 1989, in the city of Berlin, crowds gathered along the Berlin Wall.

A DIVIDED CITY

fter World War II, the leading Allied powers (France, Britain, the Soviet Union, and the United States) divided Germany into eastern and western halves. West Germany remained a capitalist nation—that is, a nation that allowed private enterprise. It also became a democracy—a nation that gave its citizens a voice in running their own government. West Germany allied itself with the United States and the nations of Western Europe. East Germany became a Communist nation, tightly controlled by the Soviet Union.

The Allies also split the German capital of Berlin into eastern and western halves. Britain, France, and the United States controlled the western half, while the Soviets controlled the eastern half. West Berlin was a democratic, capitalist city. Its citizens were allowed to travel freely to West Germany. But Berlin as a whole was located entirely within East Germany, which meant that West Berlin was a democratic island surrounded by a Communist nation.

Frequently, East Germans tried to escape from East Berlin into West Berlin. From there, they could travel to Western Europe and live freely. To stop this migration, in 1961 the East German government built a high concrete wall, topped with barbed wire and patrolled by troops, around West Berlin. The Berlin Wall helped prevent East German citizens from escaping their nation.

Workers construct a concrete wall in 1961 to separate East Berlin from West Berlin.

In November 1989, border guards watch as demonstrators chip away at the Berlin Wall, a concrete barrier that separated East and West Germany for twenty-eight years.

As crowds began to tear down the wall, police officers stood by without interfering—a sign that government authority was crumbling. Other protesters broke into government buildings and destroyed government posters and statues.

East German protesters also lashed out at the Soviet Union, which had long held a tight grip on their government. In Dresden, demonstrators surrounded KGB headquarters and threatened to ransack the building and take the KGB agents prisoner. Vladimir Putin was inside the headquarters when the crowds began to gather.

The KGB did not want it known that the Soviet Union had been spying on private East German citizens. Agents did not want their methods of information gathering revealed to the public. So within the building, Putin and his colleagues worked furiously to destroy their files, burning thousands of top-secret documents and photographs.

As the crowd grew angrier, Putin called Moscow for instructions. But his bosses gave him no guidance or orders. The KGB agents in Dresden were on their own. Putin realized that the Soviet government was growing weak. It was unwilling to use military force against the protesters. The once-powerful Soviet army and KGB were crumbling.

NEW DIRECTIONS

With the fall of the Berlin Wall, the KGB withdrew from East Germany. Vladimir Putin and his family returned to the Soviet Union. The fall of the wall also sent a signal to Soviet leaders in Moscow: without a massive wall and guard towers staffed twenty-four hours a day, the Communists could do nothing to prevent the people of Berlin from going where they wanted, when they wanted. In turn, the Soviet Union was losing control of all of East Germany and the other nations of Communist Europe.

Earlier in 1989, the Soviet army had suffered a defeat in Afghanistan, a Central Asian nation bordering the Soviet Union to the south. The powerful

As the Soviet Union's power began to weaken, it pulled its troops out of Afghanistan, left, where they had been stationed since 1979 to support a struggling Communist government there.

Soviet military had invaded the country to support a Communist leader there, but Afghan fighters had inflicted heavy casualties (death and injury) on the Soviets. The defeat sent shock waves through Soviet society. Suddenly, the Soviet superpower seemed weak and ineffective.

The KGB offered Vladimir Putin a new job in Moscow, but he turned down the offer. Putin understood that an important change was coming to the Soviet Union. He knew that his life as a spy was coming to an end and that he would have to change directions. In an interview, he later said, "I knew there was no future to the [Communist] system. The country didn't have a future. And it would have been very difficult to sit inside the system and wait for it all to collapse around me."

CAREER CHANGE

Putin didn't leave the KGB right away, however. He took an undercover job at Leningrad State University. In this position, he worked as a spy, watching students, professors, and visitors from abroad and passing information about their activities to his bosses. To disguise this secret work, he also held a job at the university, as assistant to university president Stanislav Merkuriev. In this way, he was able to carry on his spying from inside the president's office. No one suspected that he worked for the KGB.

Putin was happy to be back at the university. He wanted to make a career change and knew he could make professional connections at the school. Soon a former professor introduced Putin to Anatoly Sobchak, chairman of the Leningrad City Council. Sobchak needed assistants to help him govern the city, and he offered Putin a job.

As a man who had traveled abroad and spoke fluent German, Putin felt he could be useful in city government. Only one thing worried him—his former career in the KGB. As opposition to the Soviet system grew, KGB agents were growing more and more unpopular. If Sobchak hired Putin, the city risked a

In the early 1990s, Putin, second from left, *was appointed to a position with the Leningrad City Council. He worked under Anatoly Sobchak,* center shaking hands, *the chairman of the council.*

public outcry. Putin's work as a spy both at home and abroad would be held up to close investigation.

To work for the city, Putin would have to cut all his connections to the KGB. What's more, a city government career offered much less security than a job with the KGB. Nevertheless, Putin moved ahead. With the approval of his KGB bosses, he resigned completely from the KGB. He even arranged for a television interview in which he discussed his KGB career frankly. That way, his past—his work as a secret agent—was an open book, and no one could use it to discredit him in the future.

Putin's new position was head of the Committee for Foreign Liaison with the city government. In this job, he worked with foreign governments and companies that wanted to do business in Leningrad. He helped foreign banks open branches in the city, and he set up special investment zones, where foreign companies could operate factories and offices. Soon U.S. companies such as Coca-Cola, Gillette, and Wrigley opened offices in Leningrad.

With this work, Putin and other Russians were beginning a transition from the Communist form of business to a capitalist model. Private banks, stock exchanges, and other economic organizations were brand new to Russia. In helping foreign businesses open, Putin and other city officials learned about capitalism on the job. In one of his first accomplishments, Putin helped bring a fiber-optic cable and high-tech phone service to Leningrad.

Soviet leader Mikhail Gorbachev (wearing hat) speaks to the press on March 17, 1991, after casting his ballot in a national referendum (vote). The referendum asked for more self-government in the fifteen Soviet republics.

Chapter **FOUR**

END OF A SUPERPOWER

THE SOVIET UNION CONTINUED TO BE ROCKED BY economic turmoil. Citizens faced ever more severe food and housing shortages. Farms and businesses continued to fail. More people began to go hungry. Citizens, fed up with the failures of the Soviet system, demanded change.

In June 1990, Russia, the largest and most powerful of the Soviet republics, declared that its own laws took priority over those passed by the Soviet government. Throughout the remainder of the year, each of the fourteen other Soviet republics made similar declarations. In July 1991, Mikhail Gorbachev signed treaties giving Russia and nine other republics partial self-government. The Soviet Union seemed to be falling apart. It was also losing its allies in Eastern Europe. One by one, Communist governments—in East Germany, Poland, Hungary, Czechoslovakia, Bulgaria, and Romania—fell like dominoes.

DESPERATE MEASURES

Within the Communist Party, powerful leaders grew fearful and angry. They blamed Mikhail Gorbachev for their country's weakness, for its economic problems, and for the disintegration of the Soviet empire. They decided on desperate action: the overthrow of Gorbachev and a coup d'etat, or seizure of power. One of the coup leaders was Vladimir Kryuchkov, head of the KGB.

In the early morning hours of August 19, 1991, the plotters went into action. Kryuchkov and his companions sent military officers to Mikhail Gorbachev's dacha (country house) in Foros, on the shores of the Black Sea. The officers offered Gorbachev the chance to cooperate with them. When Gorbachev refused, the plotters placed him and his family under house arrest, keeping them captive in their own dacha.

The coup leaders then declared a national state of emergency. With this order, they banned all protests and political meetings; shut down newspapers, radio broadcasts, and TV stations; and threatened to set a curfew (a deadline for citizens to go home at night). They hoped to suppress all dissent, repeal Gorbachev's reforms, and reclaim tight government control by the

Russian citizens line up in the streets of Moscow to resist a coup attempt by Soviet hard-liners in August 1991.

Communists. Kryuchkov signed arrest warrants, ordering the police to pick up seventy people who he knew or believed would oppose the coup. He ordered tanks and soldiers into the streets of Moscow to keep order.

When the coup began, Vladimir Putin and his family were on vacation in the countryside. As soon as Putin heard about the coup attempt, he rushed back to Leningrad. He met Sobchak and other city officials at their offices in the Smolny Institute. Confusion and fear reigned in the streets, on television, and on the radio. No one was quite sure what was happening in Moscow—or whether the military had taken sides in the coup attempt. Sobchak and his aides went into

Russian president Boris Yeltsin, center, holding paper, *speaks to a crowd of protesters from atop a tank in Moscow on August 19, 1991. Yeltsin encouraged the crowd to resist the Communist hard-liners, who had staged a coup in an effort to restore the Soviet Union to stricter Communist rule.*

the streets to rally people against the coup. It was clear to Putin and Sobchak that most people opposed the coup and that at least in Leningrad, the plotters would have a fight on their hands.

Boris Yeltsin, the newly elected Russian president, returned from his country dacha to deal with the emergency in Moscow. He climbed atop a tank in front of the Russian parliament building to rally opposition to the coup. The acting mayor of Moscow, Yuri Luzhkov, joined Yeltsin and called for the people of Moscow to resist the coup. Thousands of people took to the streets, holding rallies and defying the coup leaders to attack them. The soldiers in their tanks made no effort to subdue the protesters.

The plotters soon discovered that they had little support among the public, soldiers, or military officers.
The coup quickly collapsed, and Mikhail Gorbachev
returned to Moscow safely. The Soviet government
arrested several of the coup leaders, while Yeltsin
banned the Communist Party from participating further in the Russian government.

Yeltsin's actions against the coup plotters made him a
hero, while Gorbachev resumed his place at the head of
the Soviet government. But it was too late to save the
Soviet Union. The coup attempt—and the fall of other
Communist governments in Eastern Europe—inspired
several Soviet republics to declare their full independence from the Soviet Union. In December 1991,
Mikhail Gorbachev resigned, and the Soviet government
collapsed. The fifteen republics of the Soviet Union,
including Russia, all became independent nations.

The KGB was disbanded in late 1991. The Soviet
Communist Party ceased operations around the same
time. Vladimir Putin took his Communist Party membership card out of his wallet and put it in a drawer
at home. And his hometown of Leningrad reverted to
its old, pre-Communist name, Saint Petersburg.

HOLDING RUSSIA TOGETHER

After the collapse of the Soviet Union, Russia became
the Russian Federation, the largest country in the
world. The federation spanned eleven time zones and
two continents, from the Baltic Sea in the west to the

Pacific Ocean in the east, from the Arctic Ocean southward to the deserts and mountains of Central Asia. Russian leaders wrote a new constitution, which allowed people to form different political parties, elect a president, and elect a legislature.

The birth of a new, democratic Russia did not bring about peace and prosperity, however. With the collapse of the Soviet system, the state could no longer guarantee people jobs. Thousands of state-run businesses were shut down or sold to private buyers, and millions of Russians found themselves out of work. Schools and government offices closed. Roads and bridges went without repairs, power plants stopped working, and aging trains and airplanes broke down, causing hundreds of deadly accidents. Inflation (rising prices) skyrocketed. Even those with jobs could barely afford to buy food and household goods.

To make matters worse, police offices shut down, and law enforcement all but disappeared. Criminal gangs arose in all Russia's major cities and took over the operation of businesses, large and small. To avoid trouble with the government, gang leaders bribed officials to allow them to operate as they pleased. Corruption ran riot in government offices.

At the same time, the former Soviet army, which had once intimidated much of the world, grew weak. There was no more Soviet empire to defend, and the new Russian government had little money to pay soldiers or maintain equipment. Many soldiers lived in poor conditions, and many went hungry when their salaries were unpaid.

The Russian Federation was a patchwork quilt of administrative regions and different ethnic groups. Most people were ethnically Russians, but others were Tatars, Chechens, and members of other ethnic minorities. In the district of Chechnya in southern Russia, some people wanted total independence for their region. Chechen fighters formed their own army and began to wage war against the Russian government. Boris Yeltsin and other leaders feared that the Chechen demand for independence would inspire other ethnic groups to try to break off from Russia as well. If this occurred, it seemed likely that Russia would be torn completely apart.

Yeltsin also faced trouble within his own administration. In 1993 two of his political rivals, Alexander Rutskoi and Ruslan Khasbulatov, led a movement against him in the Russian legislature. When the conflict turned violent, Yeltsin had the men arrested. He retained his office, but it was clear that he and the new Russian Federation faced difficult days ahead.

Putin, right, *became a part of the new, democratically elected government of Saint Petersburg in 1992 when Sobchak,* left, *was elected mayor of the city.*

Chapter **FIVE**

REACHING THE
KREMLIN

THROUGHOUT THE TRANSITION TO RUSSIAN INDEPEN-
dence, Vladimir Putin kept his position in the Saint
Petersburg city government. In 1992 he helped Saint
Petersburg make the switch from Communism to
democracy. He and other city leaders felt that Saint
Petersburg should have a democratically elected
mayor instead of an appointed city council chairman.
They set up elections, and Putin's boss, Anatoly
Sobchak, won the mayor's job.

As a foreign liaison for the city, Putin met important
people from Europe and the United States, including
new U.S. vice president Al Gore. In 1994 he welcomed
two more famous Americans, media owner Ted Turner
and his wife, actress Jane Fonda, to his offices. Turner

and Fonda had come to Russia to plan the Goodwill Games, an international athletic competition much like the Olympics, that was scheduled for Saint Petersburg in 1994.

Because Putin held an important job in city government, the family enjoyed a comfortable life. They were able to afford a car and their own apartment in Saint Petersburg. They had also begun construction of

FIRE AT THE DACHA

The Putin family spent six years building a dacha outside Saint Petersburg. The home was spacious, with two levels. On the second floor, a balcony offered a view of the surrounding forest and a nearby lake. On the first floor, Putin installed a *banya*, a traditional Russian sauna.

In the summer of 1996, the house was finally finished. The Putins moved in their furniture, clothing, books, and housewares, and settled in. For six weeks, they enjoyed the comforts of their new home in the peaceful countryside. Putin loved to sweat in the hot banya, then run to a nearby stream for a cold swim. Katya and Masha found endless games to play in the woods and at the small lake nearby.

On one occasion, Putin invited his secretary, Marina Yentaltseva, and her husband and daughter to the dacha. While the women talked and the children played, Putin and Marina's husband retreated to the banya. After working up a sweat, they went outside to the stream and jumped in. Refreshed, they returned to the house through the banya.

their own dacha about sixty miles from Saint Petersburg. The girls were growing up. Masha, then aged nine, and Katya, aged eight, enjoyed playing with Barbie dolls and the family dog, a sheepdog named Malysh. Forty-one-year-old Putin still practiced judo in his free time. In March 1994, Mayor Sobchak promoted Putin, appointing him deputy (assistant) mayor of Saint Petersburg.

When he entered the banya, Putin heard a sudden noise. Then he saw flames crawling up the banya's walls and along the ceiling. He ran into the house and shouted for everyone to get out. Everyone managed to escape but Masha, who was trapped in her room on the second floor. Putin rushed up and encouraged his frightened daughter to climb out the window on a makeshift rope made of bedsheets. But she was too scared to move, so he dropped her over the balcony to the others waiting below. Then he jumped off the balcony himself.

After a few terrible minutes, as the Putins saw all their possessions destroyed, a fire brigade arrived. But the firefighters did not have enough water in their trucks to save the house, and they did not have a hose long enough to reach the lake. The new dacha quickly burned to the ground.

Putin ordered an investigation, which found that faulty construction of the sauna had led to the fire. The Putins would not give up on their country dacha, however. They began building a new one, exactly the same as the old one, but with one important difference—the builders placed the banya outside, well away from the house.

The family had a terrible scare in 1994 when a driver ran a red light and smashed into Lyudmila and Katya, who were driving in the family car through the busy streets of Saint Petersburg. Katya was unhurt, but Lyudmila was knocked unconscious. An ambulance took her to the October 25th Hospital, the city's main trauma center. There, she endured two operations to repair cracks in her spine and skull. Her recovery was slow but complete, and after several months, life returned to normal for the Putins.

On the national scene, Russia continued to be plagued by economic and political strife. In Chechnya the independence movement grew stronger. In December 1994, President Yeltsin sent forty thousand troops to crush the rebellion. Violence raged in Chechnya's cities, and thousands of civilians were killed.

A Chechen woman surveys the destruction caused by the Russian bombing of the Chechen capital of Grozny in December 1994.

Kremlin buildings stand behind a high fortress wall. Putin came to work in the Kremlin in 1996. While the Kremlin has been the seat of power in Moscow since the 1100s, most of the existing Kremlin structures were built in the 1400s.

STEPPING UP

Back in Saint Petersburg, in 1996 Mayor Sobchak lost his bid for reelection. The new mayor, Vladimir Yakovlev, asked Putin to stay on as deputy mayor. But Putin didn't want to work for Yakovlev, against whom he had campaigned in the elections. He resigned from his job, uncertain what the future might bring.

Also in 1996, Boris Yeltsin ran for reelection as president of Russia. Putin admired Yeltsin and worked on his behalf, helping run Yeltsin's campaign headquarters in Saint Petersburg. Yeltsin won the election with a lot of help from several television networks and newspapers that gave him favorable press.

Shortly after the election, in August 1996, President Yeltsin's chief of staff, Pavel Borodin, offered Putin a job as his assistant. Putin accepted the position. The family moved to Moscow, and Putin went to work in the Kremlin. The massive fortress had served as the

President Yeltsin, left, *watched Putin as he worked in the new Yeltsin administration.*

seat of power in czarist Russia and in the Communist Soviet Union, and again in the new democratic Russia.

Working in Moscow, Putin had several opportunities to meet President Yeltsin. Putin admired Yeltsin for his energy and charisma. In turn, Yeltsin saw Putin as a clear-thinking, hardworking official who stuck by his principles. Putin's calm demeanor impressed Yeltsin most of all. It seemed that nothing could shake Putin's confidence or self-control.

In 1997 Putin's qualities and experience earned him a promotion to a new position, head of Russia's Main Control Directorate. This big department kept a watch on government employees and operations. Its job was to make sure the government operated as honestly and efficiently as possible. This was a very large task in post-Communist Russia, where bribery, cheating, and lawlessness were rampant in government and private business.

In 1998 Putin moved up again, becoming first deputy head of Yeltsin's presidential administration. In this job, he dealt with the governors of Russia's different regions and saw firsthand how these regions operated. He saw that some governors were hardworking and fair but that others ran their territories like dictators. They did what they pleased and ignored the federal government in Moscow as much as possible.

Putin believed that all governors should follow national laws and obey orders from Moscow without question. He believed in the principle of *vertikal,* or the strict vertical (top-to-bottom) governance of Russia. This principle meant that nobody worked independently, that every official took orders from the bosses above, and that everyone followed directions from the capital. Putin believed that vertikal was the only way for the patchwork quilt of the Russian Federation to hold together.

HEAD OF THE FSB

In 1998 another promotion came for Vladimir Putin. Boris Yeltsin appointed him head of the FSB (Federalnaya Sluzbha Bezopasnosti—or Federal Security Service), the Russian intelligence agency that had replaced the Soviet-era KGB. This was one of the most powerful jobs in Russia. The FSB had access to all the files, all the information, and all the secrets collected by the KGB during the Communist era. Yeltsin believed Putin would not abuse his authority by using the files against his enemies or to strike fear in Russian citizens. In Yeltsin's eyes, Putin had a very strong and sure moral compass. As Yeltsin wrote about Putin:

> He did not allow himself to be manipulated in political games. Even I was amazed by his solid moral code. . . . For Putin, the single criterion [standard] was the morality of a given action or the decency of a given person. He would not do anything that conflicted with his understanding of honor. He was always prepared to part with his high post if his sense of integrity would require it.

In fact, Yeltsin had already decided on Putin as the best man, eventually, to serve as the prime minister of Russia. (In Russia, citizens vote for their president, the head of the nation. The president then appoints the prime minister, who handles day-to-day government operations.) But it was too early for such a move. Yeltsin knew that the appointment of an obscure former KGB agent to such an important post would raise an outcry. In Yeltsin's strategy, Putin would head the FSB. The public would have a chance to see him on television, listen to him speak, and get used to him. In this way, Yeltsin would prepare Russia for Vladimir Putin as prime minister.

But the appointment as head of the FSB did not please Vladimir Putin or his family. It meant returning to his old way of life, when his work required secrecy and every move involved careful planning. In an interview, he recalled:

> I remember coming into the KGB building where I worked and feeling as if they were plugging me into an electrical outlet. I don't know, maybe I was the only one who felt that way, but I think the majority of people who worked there did too. It put you in a constant state of tension. All the papers are secret. This isn't allowed, that isn't allowed.

Returning to the security agency, even though it had a new name and no longer served the Communist Party, was a lot like going into the military. In the FSB, everyone had orders to follow. Once in while, the agency did a thorough investigation of its own members, just to make sure agents and bosses were not doing anything illegal, dealing with criminals, or going places they should not go. Everyone had to go through the background check, even FSB head Vladimir Putin.

In addition to the frustration of returning to security work, Putin suffered a personal blow in 1998. His mother, Mariya, died of cancer that year.

YELTSIN'S DOWNFALL

Putin knew that no matter how things went in the FSB, he could count on the support of Boris Yeltsin. The president kept his high opinion of Putin, and the meetings between the two were always friendly. But Yeltsin was in poor health. Through the late 1990s, he grew sicker and frailer each year. He had several heart attacks and spent much of his time recovering in hospital beds. He did not appear in public very often. When he did appear on television, he looked unsteady and confused. Inside the Kremlin, Yeltsin was too weak to make important decisions. A small group of friends and family made all the decisions for him.

But this group had no experience managing a government or leading a country. Nobody had elected them to any public office. Their only claim to power was their friendship with or family ties to Boris Yeltsin. As Yeltsin's strength and authority ebbed, some of his staff stole money from the public treasury, took bribes from business owners, ordered public prosecution (trials) of their enemies, and lived like kings and queens. In the meantime, the Russian economy crumbled further, and the people grew even poorer.

In 1999, as Boris Yeltsin grew weaker, the people around him began asking a difficult question. Who would be the next president of Russia? Yeltsin and his aides wanted to determine the answer to this question ahead of time, because they were afraid of what might happen after they left office. The next president might turn against them and put them on trial for corruption. They might have to leave the country and go into exile in Europe. Or they might go to jail.

In early 1999, Yevgeny Primakov was Russia's prime minister. Primakov was an experienced and influential politician, a holdover from the last Soviet government of the 1980s. But Yeltsin did not trust Primakov. He knew Primakov was an ambitious man who wanted to be the next president of Russia. Threatened by Primakov's independence and ambition, Yeltsin fired him and appointed Sergei Stepashin in his place.

Vladimir Putin and Stepashin knew each other well. In the early 1990s, Stepashin had headed the FSB in Saint Petersburg. Putin respected Stepashin and supported him as prime minister. As it turned out, however, Yeltsin did not see eye to eye with Stepashin on many issues. Yeltsin quickly grew disenchanted with Stepashin and unsure of his loyalty.

By this time, family and friends were surrounding Yeltsin like vultures. They were taking advantage of the president's poor health and mental confusion to grab whatever power and privileges they could. A new presidential election was approaching in the spring of

2000, and according to Russian law, Yeltsin could not run for another term. Looking around for a satisfactory replacement, Yeltsin cast his eye on Vladimir Putin.

Yeltsin knew that Putin was a reliable official who ably carried out orders from his superiors. Also, at aged forty-seven, Putin was young and energetic, not an old man. Yeltsin, aged sixty-eight, admired Putin's youth. He knew that Russia had been ruled for many years by old and frail men who could not inspire the young people who represented Russia's future.

In August 1999, Yeltsin fired Sergei Stepashin and appointed Vladimir Putin as the new prime minister of Russia. This appointment caught the Russian people

President Yeltsin, right, *meets with his new acting prime minister, Vladimir Putin,* left, *in August 1999.*

by surprise. Most of them knew nothing about Vladimir Putin. But they did know that Putin did not belong to any powerful political party. He had no mass of powerful supporters, such as businessmen who depended on him for favors. Russia had many corrupt leaders. To citizens, Vladimir Putin seemed cleaner than most. To Boris Yeltsin, the appointment of Putin as prime minister was the next step in moving Putin into place to take over the Russian presidency.

Prime Minister Putin faced tough decisions regarding the growing conflict in Chechnya in the summer of 1999.

Chapter **SIX**

INTO THE DEEP END

A FEW DAYS AFTER PUTIN BECAME PRIME MINISTER, his father died in Saint Petersburg. He had little time to mourn, however. In the late summer of 1999, the Chechnya conflict began to flare up again. Chechen separatists massed on the border of Dagestan, a neighboring territory, and then invaded. In August bombs destroyed several large apartment buildings in Moscow. Several hundred people were killed, and many more were injured. The Russian government blamed the bombings on Chechen rebels. It labeled them terrorists—people who use violence to frighten civilians and to pressure governments into giving in to their political demands.

An Iron Fist

Enraged by the challenge to the Russian government, Prime Minister Putin ordered military attacks on the Chechens and made the following statement: "In blowing up the houses of our fellow citizens, the bandits are blowing up the state. They are undermining authority—not of the president, city, or Duma [legislature]. But of authority [itself]."

Putin ordered the Russian army to invade Chechnya on September 30, 1999. The public was firmly behind Putin in this war, although legally it was not a war at all. Because the invasion was called an

A Russian tank guards the border between Russia and Chechnya to prevent Chechen refugees from crossing into Russia. These refugees were fleeing violence between Chechen rebels and Russian troops sent to the region by Putin in September 1999.

antiterrorist operation, Putin did not have to ask the legislature for a declaration of war or a national state of emergency.

Chechnya: A Long History of Rebellion

Chechnya is located in the northern Caucasus Mountains in southern Russia. Its people are mostly Muslims. That is, they practice Islam, a religion that has roots in the Middle East.

The Russian Empire conquered Chechnya in 1859. But the Chechen people did not want to be part of Russia. For one thing, their religion, Islam, set them apart from other Russians, who were mostly Christians. The Chechens wanted to govern themselves, independent of Russian control. Several times over the years, Chechen rebels struck out at Russian forces.

After the Russian Revolution, Chechnya continued to resist control by the government of the Soviet Union. During World War II, Soviet leader Joseph Stalin accused the Chechens of disloyalty. Believing Chechens might take up arms against the Soviet army, Stalin transported hundreds of thousands of Chechens to remote settlements in Central Asia. The government then gave Chechen land and homes to settlers from other parts of the Soviet Union. The Chechens were not allowed to return to their homeland until 1957.

The Chechens did not forget their mistreatment by the Russians and the Soviets. In 1991, when the Soviet Union broke apart, the Chechens saw an opportunity to seek their independence once more. They began to fight against the new Russian government.

The war served to increase Putin's popularity. The Moscow bombings had frightened the Russian people. On top of rising crime and poverty, they now had terrorism to fear. They wanted something done about the situation, and an outright war on the Chechens to crush the rebellion once and for all seemed like a good solution.

Boris Yeltsin also believed that ordinary Russians supported Putin's tough stand on Chechnya. Yeltsin explained:

> I am convinced that the reason for Putin's popularity was that he instilled hope, faith, and a sense of protection and calm. He didn't talk big, but he reacted to situations the way tens of millions of Russians reacted to them, with honesty and toughness. Putin gave people a guarantee of personal security backed by the state. People believed that he, personally, could protect them. That's what explains his surge in popularity. . . . Putin got rid of Russia's fear. And Russia repaid him with profound gratitude.

Some people argued that the Chechen fight for independence was a noble cause—no different from the independence movements that had occurred earlier in Russia and the other former Soviet republics. But Putin believed the Chechen rebels represented a serious threat to Russia. "I have never for a second believed . . . that Chechnya would limit itself to its own independence," he said. "It would become a beachhead [stepping-stone] for further attacks on Russia." He believed that if granted independence, the Chechens would try to swallow up more territory, and the whole Russian Federation would disintegrate.

Convinced he was correct, Putin did not appreciate any criticism of Russia's actions in Chechnya. Even journalists, whose job it was to report news, should keep quiet, Putin thought, and not criticize the government or the army in a time of war. One journalist, Andrei Babitsky, particularly bothered Putin. Babitsky, a radio reporter, sent detailed dispatches from the battlefields of Chechnya to Moscow's Radio Liberty. Babitsky told about Russian forces killing civilians and committing other atrocities. He was openly critical of the war and the government's handling of the Chechnya crisis.

Reporter Andrei Babitsky was jailed for his uncensored coverage of the crisis in Chechnya in 1999.

Putin decided that his government did not have to put up with Babitsky's embarrassing reports. The police accused Babitsky of spying for the Chechens, arrested him, and imprisoned him. They also seized his video interviews with Chechen civilians. Eventually, the government dropped the charges against Babitsky, but his treatment was severe enough to warn other journalists not to criticize the government.

VERTICAL POWER

Yeltsin could see that Putin was becoming more and more popular with the Russian people. He felt it was a good time to step down and turn over the reins of government to his young colleague. On New Year's Eve 1999, Yeltsin announced his retirement and appointed Vladimir Putin as Russia's temporary president.

But to officially become president, Putin had to win the upcoming election. His supporters formed the Unity Party to back his presidential campaign. Among his several opponents was former prime minister Yevgeny Primakov, running with the Fatherland Party. Primakov and his ally Yuri Luzhkov, the mayor of Moscow, were insiders, men who had taken advantage of the changes in Russian government to advance their own power. They also represented a threat to Boris Yeltsin, who feared they would charge him with corruption after he left office.

On May 7, 2000, Putin was inaugurated in the Kremlin in Moscow as Russia's second democratically elected president. He took over from Boris Yeltsin, who stepped down on December 31, 1999.

Compared to Luzhkov and Primakov, Putin was a newcomer, an obscure outsider who appeared hard-working and honest. Seeing the polls (surveys of voters' preferences) going against him, Primakov withdrew from the race in February 2000. Putin became the clear favorite and easily won the election in the next month.

Putin did not like disorder, confusion, or uncertainty. But he was leading a country that was going through one of the most chaotic times in its history, a time when nobody seemed confident in the future or the proper path for Russian society to take. Should this enormous country follow a Western model (similar to Western Europe and the United States), in which people were guaranteed rights, businesses operated freely, and government power was limited? Or should Russia stick with a traditional Russian system, in which a powerful leader ruled largely through force, curbing freedoms and exercising control wherever he saw fit?

Putin favored the old-fashioned approach. He believed in a strong central government and a powerful leader. He was willing to take away people's freedoms and, if necessary, use the law against those who opposed him. He was determined to establish vertikal. Putin wanted clear lines of authority between Moscow and the governments of the twenty-one republics and sixty oblasts (subdivisions) into which the Russian Federation was divided.

He took an important first step on May 13, 2000, a week after his formal inauguration as president. He wrote a decree, or presidential order, that established seven areas known as *okrugs* on the map of Russia. A governor, not elected but rather appointed by the president, would oversee each okrug. Each governor would make sure that leaders within the republics and oblasts kept themselves in line, followed Moscow's orders, and did not claim too much independence from Putin's government.

Putin's next step was to get control of both houses of the legislature in Moscow. He wrote a new law that weakened the Federation Council, the upper house of the Russian legislature. The law allowed Putin's regional governors (whom he appointed) to select half the council members, while the other half were selected by regional legislatures. In this way, Putin ensured that at least half the Federation Council shared his political views. The Duma, or lower house, was elected by the people. But Duma members saw Putin's popularity and passed his new laws without much opposition.

Few government officials or legislators made any protest against these actions. One exception was Boris Berezovsky, a member of the Duma who owned television networks and newspapers. One of the wealthiest men in Russia, Berezovsky criticized Putin and

While most members of the Duma supported Putin's legislation, Boris Berezovsky challenged the new president.

charged that the new president was trying to make himself a dictator. Berezovsky also sharply criticized the war in Chechnya. He believed that Putin should open peace talks with the Chechen rebels and try to bring the war to an end.

In May Berezovsky wrote a letter to President Putin. The letter attacked Putin for his antidemocratic ways and his heavy-handed rule. The two men then met to try to hammer out their differences. But Berezovsky soon realized that he would not win this battle. There was no point in arguing with Vladimir Putin about laws, government, and personal freedoms in Russia. In an interview, Berezovsky later said:

> [Putin] said he still believed that we had to build a liberal democratic state in Russia . . . but we had to do it by force, because people were not ready for it. Putin believes everything has to be governed from above, so it is necessary to concentrate power, concentrate the mass media, and to rule business.

In protest against Putin's policies, Berezovsky resigned his seat in the Duma on July 17. But Berezovsky had very little support from the public. To most people, he was just another rich man who operated above the law. Putin, on the other hand, had a very different public image. He seemed to be a hard-working family man, a man with Russia's interests and not his own at heart. He seemed to care little for enriching himself.

Russians enthusiastically supported their new president. They were tired of all the confusion and disorder that had reigned in Russia since the collapse of the Soviet Union. They were highly suspicious of wealthy individuals like Berezovsky. They were glad to be rid of the unsteady, unhealthy Boris Yeltsin. They wanted a sure, strong hand at the top, and it seemed they had finally found one in President Putin.

THE *KURSK* DISASTER

In the summer of 2000, Vladimir Putin was riding high as the new president of Russia. He had support among the public. He had control over the Russian legislature, which would do nothing without his approval. He was fighting the dangerous Chechens, whipping the regional leaders into line, and facing down corrupt officials and business owners.

As president, Putin had learned the ropes quickly. But as a politician, he did not feel confident. Never before in his career had he needed to care about the mood of the people or the opinions of voters. He was not sure how to act in public or how to react to sudden, unexpected events. Then a tragic situation involving the Russian submarine *Kursk* put his public relations skills to a difficult test.

The nuclear-powered *Kursk* was the most advanced vessel in the Russian submarine fleet. Built during the

Soviet era, it represented the technological advances and successes of Soviet science and engineering. But the *Kursk* carried with it a serious, dangerous flaw. The vibration of the submarine while moving underwater could accidentally set off its own torpedoes. This flaw had never been investigated or corrected.

On August 12, 2000, while the submarine was on maneuvers in the Barents Sea north of Russia, one of its torpedoes accidentally exploded. Damaged from the explosion, the ship sank to the bottom of the sea with 118 officers and crew members trapped inside. The men began to suffocate as their supply of oxygen ran out.

The Russian navy did not have the proper equipment for a deepwater rescue operation. Finally, the navy's leaders asked for help from Norway, a nation with skilled seamen and up-to-date equipment. But the rescue operation was too late. When Norwegian divers finally reached the *Kursk* and opened its hatch to climb inside, they found the entire crew dead.

The *Kursk* disaster caught everyone in Russia by surprise. The best ship in the Russian navy had fallen to the bottom of the sea, and the navy was helpless to rescue its own sailors. People were upset that the government had to ask a foreign nation for help in saving the *Kursk*. The disaster, which received international coverage, symbolized how Russia was falling apart.

The event occurred while President Putin was enjoying a vacation in the resort of Sochi, located along the warm and sunny shores of the Black Sea. Television

President Putin, left, shakes hands with a relative of a crew member who was killed when the nuclear submarine Kursk sank to the floor of the Barents Sea in August 2000, killing all 118 sailors aboard.

cameras captured the president's relaxed mood at the time. Putin's smiles and easygoing look surprised and angered many people in Russia. It seemed to many that he did not much care about the dying sailors aboard the *Kursk*. People also grew angry at the military and at the Kremlin.

The *Kursk* disaster became a military scandal. Putin fired the navy's top commanders, and many other officers resigned their jobs. The following year, the *Kursk* was raised from the sea and the families of the dead sailors held funerals for their loved ones. Their sorrowful gatherings were broadcast to the nation, making millions of Russians wonder if their society would ever change for the better.

President Putin and First Lady Lyudmila Putin make a public appearance outside of the first family's residence in Moscow in the 1990s.

Chapter **SEVEN**

LAW AND
DISORDER

MANY RUSSIANS WERE UNEASY WITH THE STRANGE
new world they had experienced since the fall of the
Soviet Union. No longer could they count on a job
and a secure living for their families. The crime rate
was rising, and newspapers often ran stories about
corrupt government officials. The government itself
seemed adrift, often changing policies and laws without rhyme or reason.

But for a small number of Russians, life had greatly
improved since the fall of the Soviet Union. In the
chaotic 1990s, when Russia had sold off many of its
state-owned industries, some Russians had grown very
rich. They had purchased the former state companies,
sometimes bribing government officials to make shady

deals. Some of the richest Russians, such as former Duma member Boris Berezovsky, had purchased media and TV companies from the state.

Vladimir Putin didn't like media owners such as Berezovsky. He believed Russia's private television networks had deliberately made him look bad with their coverage of the *Kursk* disaster in the summer of 2000, when he was caught on film enjoying a vacation in a time of national tragedy. Putin complained to Berezovsky about this embarrassing coverage on ORT, Berezovsky's TV station. He also accused Berezovsky of financial wrongdoing and threatened to have the government take back control of ORT. Taking Putin's threats seriously, Berezovsky sold his shares (part ownership) in ORT to one of his business partners. He then left Russia and went to live in London, England.

Vladimir Gusinsky, head of the Media-Most company, had a similar experience. Gusinsky controlled NTV, another former state-run television company. One NTV show, *Kukly* (The Puppets), used puppets to make fun of Russian political leaders. For instance, in 1995 *Kukly* had ridiculed Boris Yeltsin, showing him as a drunk. (Yeltsin was, in fact, an alcoholic.)

In 2000 *Kukly* did not spare the feelings of Vladimir Putin, who was turned into a comical puppet on the show. When the government threatened to investigate NTV, the Putin puppet disappeared. Instead, the show depicted Putin as the biblical lawgiver Moses, coming down a mountain with instructions from an invisible

Putin's likeness was made into a puppet for the popular Russian TV puppet show Kukly.

but all-powerful God. The show implied that Putin thought he was a prophet like Moses, a wise man who knew more than anyone else.

Alarmed and irritated, Putin had the police raid Media-Most headquarters in June 2000. Gusinsky was arrested and thrown into jail. The government lawyer charged Media-Most with fraud for failing to repay $211 million that it owed to a government agency.

Friends and even some enemies of Gusinsky reacted with anger. In the arrest of Gusinsky, they saw Putin bringing back the old Soviet tyranny that they thought had disappeared with the end of the Soviet Union and the Communist government in 1991. On a television program, Sergei Dorenko, a reporter who had supported Putin the year before, boldly turned against him:

> We thought that the old system broke over these ten years. We dumped the robots [repressive security forces]. They have been lying there. And they stirred and started moving again, as if they heard some music. They got up and started moving. Today the security [agents] throughout the whole country are taking a message from Putin's rise to power. . . . They hear music we do not hear, and they get up like zombies and walk. They surround us. And they will go far if there is silence. . . . We need to bash them over the head every day.

Vladimir Gusinsky, head of Media-Most, was arrested in 2000.

The battle continued with Gusinsky, who was freed, then arrested again, and then freed once more. Accusations of wrongdoing were hurled back and forth. But most people in Russia supported Putin's actions against his public critics. They saw Putin as a strong leader, acting the way strong leaders in Russia had always behaved.

What's more, most people in Russia felt little sympathy for rich and powerful business owners such as Berezovsky and Gusinsky. Many Russians thought there was no way to follow the laws and rules of the country and succeed to such a degree. Therefore, they concluded, the rich must be crooked—probably working with the Russian mafia. And when Putin threatened the rich with arrest and trial, many thought his targets were simply getting what they deserved.

OLD SYMBOLS FOR A NEW RUSSIA

Russia had entered a confusing new era. It was an era of conflicting political parties—the Unity Party, the Fatherland Party, the Communist Party (which had been revived after its closure in 1991), the Liberal Democratic Party, the People's Party, and on and on. It was an era of endless debates about czarist rule, Communism, democracy, and which political system was best for Russia. Fed up with the constant debate, criticism of his policies, and what he saw as confusion, Vladimir Putin sought to impose unity and a common purpose on his nation.

In late 2000, the president asked the Duma to remain in session for one final task: the selection of Russia's official national symbols, including its state seal, national anthem, and flag. Putin had his own ideas about what those symbols should be. He proposed that a double-headed eagle, the old emblem of the Russian czar, should serve as Russia's state seal. He proposed keeping the old national anthem of the Soviet Union. He wanted Russia to adopt a white, blue, and red striped flag that had first been used after the Russian Revolution. He also suggested the old Communist flag, a red flag with the emblem of a hammer and sickle, as the official symbol of the Russian army.

Putin brought back the double-headed eagle as Russia's state seal.

Putin believed these emblems would help Russia enter the new century—and new millennium—with the many different periods of its history represented. In this way, the nation would pay respect to its past and not take sides: Communists and anti-Communists would enjoy equal standing and prestige.

But the proposed emblems also provoked a fierce debate in Russia. For many, the Communist period was a time of hunger, fear, and corruption. It was a time of dictatorship, when the state could imprison people whenever it liked. Even Boris Yeltsin spoke out against the return of the Soviet anthem.

Other people in Russia felt nostalgic for the past. They knew Communist Russia as a nation in which everyone knew his or her place. Life had been hard but predictable. Everyone had a path and knew how to follow it—whereas in the post-Communist world, life was uncertain and often downright frightening.

Despite the opposing opinions, on December 8, 2000, a large majority of the Duma agreed to adopt Putin's proposed symbols. The Federation Council also voted for the symbols. Putin had won another victory, believing that an important step toward national unity had been achieved.

NEW PARTIES AND NEW UNIONS

In early 2001, Putin was still battling Vladimir Gusinsky, who was then directing the Media-Most company and the NTV network while in exile (living abroad). In

April the government finally scored a victory. A state agency seized control of Gusinsky's empire, including NTV, the popular magazine *Itogi* (Results), and the daily newspaper *Sevodnya* (Today). The government appointed new managers and fired writers and reporters who opposed or criticized government policies. Those who remained behind knew that to keep their jobs, they would have to publicly support Vladimir Putin.

To make sure the media and journalists stayed in line, the government also formed the Media Union, a new trade union for writers. Working with government-controlled media, the Media Union set strict guidelines for employment. In return for secure jobs, members of the Media Union had to support government policies.

Politicians supporting Putin also created a new political party called Edinaya Rossiya, or United Russia. The first party that had formed to support Putin's presidential campaign, the Unity Party, shut itself down, as did the Fatherland Party, which had opposed Putin in the elections of 2000. Putin convinced former Fatherland Party leaders Yuri Luzhkov and Yevgeny Primakov to join the United Russia Party, a signal to their followers that they should also accept Putin's leadership.

Creation of the United Russia Party ended the independence of Putin's strongest opponents and made them partners with Vladimir Putin in the new government. The party also formed a strong majority in the Duma and the Federation Council, making it nearly impossible for any lawmakers to oppose Putin.

Young people of the group Walking Together show their support for President Putin at a rally in Moscow.

Putin knew that the most troublesome critics of government and the state had always been young people. He dealt with this potential problem by creating an official youth organization known as Walking Together. Members of this group enjoyed important privileges—such as trips abroad and the right to attend special events—that nonmembers did not have. But they were also expected to remain obedient to the government and president and show their support by attending public rallies.

Through the new media union, political party, and youth organization, Putin hoped to create a more unified and largely obedient public in the new Russia. But he also knew that public support could vanish with economic hard times or political scandals.

Putin shakes hands with U.S. president George W. Bush. Putin thought it was important to continue to improve relations with the United States, Russia's former enemy in the Cold War.

Chapter **EIGHT**

FACING DOWN
TERRORISM

RELATIONS WITH THE UNITED STATES HAD ALWAYS
been crucial to Soviet leaders. After the fall of the
Soviet Union, the United States stood alone as the
world's only superpower. Mikhail Gorbachev and Boris
Yeltsin had improved relations with the United States
somewhat. But the new Russia was weak and divided,
and it was easy prey for the military and economic
power of its former enemy.

Putin had to decide how to approach the United
States. Should Russia keep up friendly relations and
cooperate with the United States? Should Russia try to
join the North Atlantic Treaty Organization (NATO), a
military alliance formed after World War II and led by
the United States (even though NATO was originally

designed to defend Europe against a Soviet invasion)? Or should Russia build new alliances of its own, pursuing its own interests in Europe and Asia without paying any heed to what the United States wanted?

The right answer was not clear. Putin had been trained as a KGB spy, and the KGB had always seen the United States as an enemy. He could not completely ignore his training, but he also knew that Russia would benefit from good relations with the United States.

In early 2001, Putin put out friendly words to the new U.S. president, George W. Bush. Putin praised the new Bush administration and expressed hope for better relations between the two nations. But the Bush administration did not return these friendly sentiments. In fact, President Bush paid little attention to Russia and showed little concern for Russia's economic and social problems.

A FATEFUL DAY

But everything changed for Russia, the United States, and indeed the whole world on September 11, 2001. In New York City, that day began as a clear, sunny, and pleasant morning. A little after 8:00 A.M., just as the workday began, a commercial passenger jet slammed into the side of the 110-story north tower of the World Trade Center. Shortly afterward, another jet crashed into the south tower. The towers burned and then collapsed in a huge cloud of dust and smoke. A third plane hit the Pentagon, the headquarters of the

Rescue workers in New York City stand amid the devastation caused by the terrorist attacks on the World Trade Center on September 11, 2001.

U.S. military near Washington, D.C., and a fourth crashed in a field in rural Pennsylvania.

Terrorists had hijacked the four jets and used them as guided missiles to target important and symbolic buildings within the United States. The plane that crashed in Pennsylvania had probably been headed for the White House or the U.S. Capitol in Washington, D.C. But passengers had struggled with the hijackers, causing the plane to crash before it reached Washington. Roughly three thousand people died in the September 11 attacks.

Immediately afterward, President Bush declared a global war on terrorism. In a speech to the U.S. Congress, Bush declared:

> We will starve terrorists of funding, turn them one against another, drive them from place to place, until there is no refuge or no rest. And we

will pursue nations that provide aid or safe haven to terrorism. Every nation, in every region, now has a decision to make. Either you are with us, or you are with the terrorists. From this day forward, any nation that continues to harbor or support terrorism will be regarded by the United States as a hostile regime.

President Putin realized that an important moment had come for Russia. The country would have to decide how to help President Bush's "war on terrorism." The mastermind of the September 11 attacks, Osama bin Laden, leader of the terrorist al-Qaeda organization, lived in Afghanistan—on the southern borders of the old Soviet Union. Soon after the September 11 attacks, the United States demanded that the Taliban, the extremist Islamic party that ruled Afghanistan, turn over bin Laden. The United States threatened war if the Taliban did not cooperate. When the Taliban refused, the United States and its allies prepared for war in Central Asia—Russia's backyard.

Putin did not hesitate. He called President Bush immediately after the attacks to express his sympathy and pledged to fully cooperate with the United States. Putin knew that the war on terrorism presented a good opportunity for Russia in its relations with the West (the United States and Western Europe). By cooperating in the war, Russia could show itself as an ally and no longer an enemy of the West.

Putin did not want Russia to fight in the war, however. He and other Russians remembered their humiliating defeat in Afghanistan in 1989. They did not want Russian soldiers going off to another war there, especially when the Chechnya conflict was still dragging on. But Russia and other former Soviet republics agreed to allow the United States to move military forces into Central Asia and to strike Afghanistan from bases there.

The war in Afghanistan began one month after the September 11 attacks. Striking Afghanistan from bases in the former Soviet republic of Uzbekistan, the United States quickly destroyed the Taliban and killed or captured many terrorists, though not bin Laden.

U.S. general Tommy Franks, right, a commander in the U.S. war on terror, briefs the press on the war in Afghanistan in December 2001. The map shows the borders shared between Afghanistan and the former Soviet republics of Turkmenistan, Uzbekistan, and Tajikstan. Russia's cooperation helped U.S. troops gain access to Afghanistan.

In the meantime, the war gave President Putin another important opportunity. On September 24, he made a speech about Chechnya and demanded that the Chechen rebels disarm within seventy-two hours. Putin said the rebels in Chechnya were terrorists, just as Osama bin Laden and his al-Qaeda organization were terrorists. He said Russia had the right to fight these terrorists with all the weapons it had. The war on terrorism would become Russia's war as well.

The Chechen rebels did not disarm, however, and the war in Chechnya continued. Putin still refused to grant the region independence. He still believed that Chechen independence would mean the disintegration of Russia. He did not want to be the president responsible for that event.

DEALS AND DISAGREEMENTS

To further improve relations with the United States and Western Europe, NATO and Russia formed the NATO-Russia Council in early 2002. The council was designed to foster military cooperation among Russia, the United States, and other NATO members.

Several months afterward, in May 2002, Putin met with President Bush in Moscow. Bush wanted to discuss Russia's huge stockpile of nuclear weapons, left over from the Soviet era. These weapons worried the United States and other nations, who feared that terrorists might find ways to acquire the nuclear bombs and other weapons.

On May 24, 2002, President Bush and President Putin spoke together at the Kremlin after signing the Strategic Offensive Reductions Treaty. In the treaty, each nation promised to drastically cut its nuclear weapons stockpiles.

At the meeting, Putin and Bush agreed to sign the Strategic Offensive Reductions Treaty. The treaty stated that the United States and Russia would dramatically cut their nuclear arsenals (stockpiles of weapons), from about 6,000 nuclear missiles each to between 1,700 and 2,200 missiles each by December 2012. This reduction would be the biggest cut in nuclear weapons in history. Not only did it promise to make the world safer, but the Moscow meeting also showed that Putin could get along with President Bush. It also proved that the United States and

Russia could work out old disagreements and sign an important treaty.

But the two leaders didn't agree on everything. In the war on terror, President Bush was not satisfied with just chasing Osama bin Laden from his Afghan bases. Bush was determined to fight terrorism by attacking states that sponsored terrorists or threatened the world with weapons of mass destruction (nuclear, chemical, or biological weapons).

With this goal, Bush ordered a rapid military buildup in the Persian Gulf region. His target was the Middle Eastern nation of Iraq, lying far to the west of Afghanistan. Bush accused Iraq of working with terrorists and building and hiding weapons of mass destruction. Bush wanted to topple Iraq's dictator, Saddam Hussein, and create a new democratic government in Iraq.

Putin and Russia watched the U.S. military buildup with alarm. For one thing, the Russian government did not want to see another war in the Middle East. It preferred that the United States use peaceful methods instead of warfare to resolve its differences with Iraq. And many Russians didn't want their government following along obediently with the United States, as it had done in cooperating with the Afghan invasion. Russians wanted their nation to act independently. So Putin knew that opposing the war in Iraq would help his popularity at home.

What's more, Putin wanted to draw his nation closer

to the countries of Western Europe, particularly France and Germany. He believed Russia could prosper by trading with these countries, selling its oil and natural gas in exchange for European consumer goods. Putin also wanted European countries to invest in Russia, which would result in more jobs and better wages for Russian workers. Officials in both France and Germany strongly opposed the war in Iraq, so it made sense for Putin to follow their lead.

So while President Bush threatened war and demanded that Iraq destroy its weapons of mass destruction, Putin asked the United States to seek a peaceful solution to the controversy. The United Nations (an international organization whose purpose is to preserve world peace and security and to help resolve disputes that could lead to war) also refused to support the invasion. But the U.S. government felt that Iraq presented an urgent threat to the United States, and President Bush moved ahead with the attack. He ordered a full-scale invasion of Iraq in March 2003.

The United States quickly occupied Iraq and in December 2003, U.S. troops captured Saddam Hussein. Then U.S. troops began the business of helping build a new, democratic Iraq. Putin said that Russia would assist in the rebuilding effort—with troops, equipment, food, and money—only if the United Nations played an important role in the process. But the United States continued its go-it-alone policy, so Russia remained on the sidelines.

On May 1, 2003, U.S. president Bush declared mission accomplished in Iraq. The conflict, however, was far from over. Despite improving relations between the United States and Russia, Putin chose to sit out the war in Iraq.

BACK FOR MORE

In late 2003, Vladimir Putin stood high in the eyes of most Russians. Most people supported his stand on Iraq and his opposition to the U.S.-led war on that country. Most also respected his attempts to draw Russia closer, politically and economically, to Western Europe.

But many Russians disliked the way Putin ruled his country with a heavy hand. He had used the threat of government trials to chase away powerful critics such as Boris Berezovsky and Vladimir Gusinsky. He had set up labor unions and youth organizations simply to create support for his own administration and his policies. He had made Russia's central government in Moscow stronger and had deliberately weakened the nation's regional governments. And he had pursued a tragic war in Chechnya that had cost thousands of lives.

The presidential election of March 14, 2004, put Putin's popularity to the test. Putin was opposed in the race by Irina Khakamada of the Union of Right Forces Party, Nikolai Kharitonov of the Communist Party, Sergei Glaziev of the Rodina Party, Oleg Malyshkin of the Liberal Democratic Party, and Sergei Mironov of the Russian Party of Life. These candidates could do little to better their chances, however, as state-controlled television stations kept their cameras focused on Putin and kept his opponents off the air.

The president had only one worry—apathy. If many voters stayed home, Putin might not get a majority of the votes needed to win the election. To get out the vote, the government lured Russians to the voting booths by offering them free concerts, reduced utility bills (such as electric and water bills), free entrance to discos, and low prices at shops near voting places.

The extensive television coverage for President Putin and the get-out-the-vote efforts worked as expected. Putin scored a landslide victory with 71.3 percent of the vote. The runner-up, Communist Nikolai Kharitonov, won just 13.7 percent. A total 64 percent of eligible voters took part in the election.

Putin and his wife, Lyudmila leave a polling station in Moscow after casting their votes in Russia's presidential election on March 14, 2004. Putin was reelected by a wide margin of victory.

After the election, Putin announced new measures meant to fight corruption in government. He proposed large increases in the pay of government workers, whose low incomes tempted them to accept bribes from crooked businesspeople. He also increased his own salary and the salaries of his top government ministers.

Putin made foreign relations a high priority. He vowed to cooperate with the European Union (EU), a political and economic federation of European countries that included among its newest members several former Soviet republics. Putin hoped that Russia and the EU would forge new business deals and cooperate closely in the war against terrorism.

MORE TERROR

In the late summer of 2004, the Chechen rebellion turned even deadlier. First, Chechen fighters bombed two passenger jets over southern Russia. Next, Chechen fighters seized a school in the Russian town of Beslan, holding hundreds of students, parents, and teachers hostage. When Russian soldiers tried to rescue the hostages, a gun battle broke out, resulting in the deaths of more than three hundred people, many of them children.

A schoolgirl in Beslan gets treated for wounds she received during the battle between Russian troops and the Chechen fighters who had seized her school in September 2004.

The Beslan attack horrified Russians and people around the world. All eyes turned to Vladimir Putin. How would he deal with the increased terrorist activity? Putin responded by reorganizing the Russian government once more. Declaring that the central government needed more authority to deal with terrorism, Putin asked the Russian legislature to pass new laws. One law stated that Russia's provincial leaders would be appointed by the president, not elected by the people. Another law said that lawmakers would take seats in the legislature based on the percentage of votes won by their political parties, not by a direct election by voters.

The new decrees raised alarm in the West about the direction of Vladimir Putin's presidency. To many observers, it seemed that Russia was returning, slowly but surely, to one-man rule and a one-party state. But Putin answered critics by pointing out that Russia is a large and difficult country to govern. More power in the central government, in his opinion, allowed a more effective fight against terrorism. It also allowed the government to rein in corrupt local officials and set down fair laws and economic policy for every region of the country. Most of all, Putin feared Russia breaking into semi-independent territories, where local governors made whatever laws they wanted. He also declared that giving any degree of independence to Chechnya would signal a dangerous victory for terrorism.

DEMOCRACY IN DOUBT

In late 2004, Vladimir Putin continued his battles with private Russian businesses. His government attacked Yukos, a giant Russian oil company, by demanding a huge payment for back taxes. Unable to make the payment, the company failed and went into bankruptcy The company's leader, Mikhail Khodorkovsky—who supported opposition political parties—was thrown in jail. Russian courts then broke up Yukos. One important part of the company was sold at auction. The buyer was Gazprom, a natural gas company owned and operated by the government of Russia. One important part of the company was sold at auction. The buyer was Rosneft, a state-owned company run by Igor Sechin—a close friend of Vladimir Putin.

Around the same time, opponents found another reason to criticize Putin. This time, democracy itself seemed to be at stake. The elections for the president of Ukraine, an important former Soviet republic, took place on November 21, 2004. Two candidates squared off: Victor Yanukovich and Victor Yushchenko.

From the Kremlin, Vladimir Putin threw his support to Yanukovich, who sought closer ties between Ukraine and Russia. Putin strongly opposed Yushchenko, who wanted more independence from Russia and closer ties with Western Europe.

The elections caused more strife than they settled. Although Yanukovich declared himself the winner, many people in Ukraine believed the elections had been rigged. They believed that many votes were phony and accused Ukrainian election officials of reporting false tallies. Thousands of Ukrainians poured into the streets to demand another election. Putin opposed the idea, claiming that the elections had been honest. Tension increased in Ukraine, where many predicted a civil war if the problem couldn't be solved.

On December 3, the Ukrainian supreme court defied Putin and Yanukovich and ordered a new election. Victor Yushchenko won this vote, held on December 26. The victory for Yushchenko was seen far and wide as a defeat for Vladimir Putin. The powerful president of Russia had tried to influence an election in a foreign country. His man had then won, likely by fraud, and then lost the recount. The Ukraine election fiasco may weaken Putin's popularity at home, draw further criticism from Europe and the West, and encourage independence movements in far-flung regions of Russia.

PUTIN AT HOME

While controversy and debate swirl around Vladimir Putin's decrees and policies, his family life remains quiet, largely unaffected by political storms. The family has a comfortable apartment in Moscow, a country home near Saint Petersburg, and another on the Black Sea. Cooks and other staff members help the Putins run their household routine.

Putin keeps in shape by practicing judo, swimming, and working out in the gym every day. The whole

Putin spars with a partner during a judo training session at the presidential residence in Moscow.

family enjoys downhill skiing, and the family dog, a toy poodle named Toska, keeps everyone company. Lyudmila Putin involves herself in many charities. She heads the Center for the Development of the Russian Language, a group dedicated to teaching the correct way to speak Russian and fighting sloppy grammar. As the president's wife, she also hosts important foreign visitors, including U.S. first lady Laura Bush, whom Lyudmila has guided to historic Russian monuments and important cultural events.

Whatever the future might hold, Vladimir Putin's career represents a remarkable change for Russia. Through a combination of energy, dedication, and luck, Putin rose from an obscure position in a massive Communist-era bureaucracy, without the benefits of strong political ties or alliances, to become the popular leader of a completely transformed nation. In the future, Russians will look back on Vladimir Putin's presidency as a turning point—a time when the Soviet past was buried once and for all and a new political era emerged in Russia.

Timeline

1952 Vladimir Vladimirovich Putin is born in Leningrad.

1961 East Germany builds the Berlin Wall to prevent East Germans from escaping to the West.

1968 Putin inquires at the Leningrad KGB office about a career as a spy.

1975 Putin graduates from the law school of Leningrad State University and enters the KGB.

1979 The Soviet army invades Afghanistan to support a Communist government there.

1983 Putin marries Lyudmila Shkrebneva, a flight attendant from Kaliningrad.

1984 Putin trains as a foreign agent at the Andropov Red Banner Institute in Moscow.

1985 The Putins' first daughter, Masha, is born. The Putins move to Dresden, East Germany, where Vladimir works as a KGB agent.

1986 The Putins' second daughter, Katya, is born.

1989 The Soviet army pulls out of Afghanistan. Protesters tear down the Berlin Wall.

1990 The Putins move back to Leningrad. Putin takes an undercover job at Leningrad State University.

1991 Boris Yeltsin becomes the first elected president of Russia. The Soviet Union collapses, and the fifteen Soviet republics become independent nations.

1992 Putin heads the Committee for Foreign Liaison in Leningrad. Russia begins to privatize, or sell off, state-owned companies and property.

1994 Putin becomes deputy mayor of Saint Petersburg. Russian troops invade Chechnya.

1996 Putin becomes deputy chief of staff for Russian president Boris Yeltsin.

1998 Putin becomes head of the FSB, Russia's new security agency.

1999 Yeltsin appoints Putin prime minister of Russia. Putin orders the second invasion of Chechnya. Yeltsin resigns and names Putin provisional president of Russia.

2000 Putin is elected president of Russia.

2001 Terrorists attack targets in the United States, and U.S. president George Bush declares a war on terrorism.

2002 Russia and NATO form the NATO-Russia Council. Putin and President Bush meet in Moscow to discuss nuclear arms reduction and the war on terrorism.

2003 The United States invades Iraq.

2004 Putin is reelected president of Russia, winning 71 percent of the vote. Chechen terrorists bomb planes and kill hostages in Russia. Putin further strengthens Russia's central government.

SOURCES

8   Vladimir Putin, *First Person: An Astonishingly Frank Self-Portrait by Russia's President*, with Nataliya Gevorkyan, Natalya Timakova, and Andrei Kolesnikov; trans. Catherine A. Fitzpatrick (New York: Public Affairs, 2000), 23.

18   Ibid., 22.

38–39   Ibid., 85–86.

58   Boris Yeltsin, *Midnight Diaries*, trans. Catherine A. Fitzpatrick (New York: Public Affairs, 2000), 329.

59   Putin, *First Person*, 131.

66   Lilia Shevtsova, *Putin's Russia* (Washington, DC: Carnegie Endowment for International Peace, 2003), 37.

68   Yeltsin, *Midnight Diaries*, 338.

68–69   David E. Hoffman, *The Oligarchs: Wealth and Power in the New Russia* (New York: Public Affairs, 2002), 486–487.

74   Ibid.

82   Ibid.

91–92   Wendy S. Ross, "U.S. to Use Every Resource to Defeat Global Terror Network, Bush Says." *U.S. Department of State, International Information Programs,* http://usinfo.state .gov/topical/pol/terror/01092080.htm. (October 13, 2003)

SELECTED BIBLIOGRAPHY

Brown, Archie, ed. *Gorbachev, Yeltsin, and Putin: Political Leadership in Russia's Transition.* Washington, DC: Carnegie Endowment for International Peace, 2001.

Herspring, Dale R., ed. *Putin's Russia: Past Imperfect, Future Uncertain.* Lanham, MD: Rowman and Littlefield Publishers, 2002.

Hoffman, David E. *The Oligarchs: Wealth and Power in the New Russia.* New York: Public Affairs, 2002.

McFaul, Michael. *Russia's Unfinished Revolution: Political Change from Gorbachev to Putin.* Ithaca, NY: Cornell University Press, 2002.

Putin, Vladimir. *First Person: An Astonishingly Frank Self-Portrait by Russia's President.* With Nataliya Gevorkyan, Natalya Timakova, and Andrei Kolesnikov. Translated by Catherine A. Fitzpatrick. New York: Public Affairs, 2000.

Rose, Richard, and Neil Munro. *Elections without Order: Russia's Challenge to Vladimir Putin.* New York: Cambridge University Press, 2002.

Shevtsova, Lilia. *Putin's Russia.* Washington, DC: Carnegie Endowment for International Peace, 2003.

Yeltsin, Boris. *Midnight Diaries.* Translated by Catherine A. Fitzpatrick. New York: Public Affairs, 2000.

FURTHER READING AND WEBSITES

BOOKS

Harvey, Miles. *The Fall of the Soviet Union.* Chicago: Children's Press, 1995.

Katz, Samuel M. *Against All Odds.* Minneapolis: Lerner Publications Company, 2005.

Márquez, Herón. *Russia in Pictures.* Minneapolis: Lerner Publications Company, 2004.

Murrell, Kathleen Berton. *Eyewitness: Russia.* New York: Dorling Kindersley, 2000.

Shields, Charles J. *Vladimir Putin.* Langhorne, PA: Chelsea House, 2002.

WEBSITES

Committee for State Security
http://www.fas.org/irp/world/russia/kgb/. This site provides an in-depth guide to the history of the KGB and its operations within the Soviet Union and in foreign nations.

The Face of Russia
http://www.pbs.org/weta/faceofrussia/. Based on a PBS television series, the site examines Russian history, politics, and culture. It includes a glossary, discussion forums, and interactive timeline.

The Moscow Times
http://www.themoscowtimes.com/indexes/01.html. This site,
produced by the most important English-language newspaper
in Russia, covers current events, business news, and cultural
highlights from Moscow and the Russian Federation.
Russian History
http://www.departments.bucknell.edu/russian/history.html.
Visitors to this site will find Russian history links, a Russian
timeline, discussion groups, archives, royal family trees, and
a wealth of other information.
Soviet Archives Exhibit
http://www.ibiblio.org/expo/soviet.exhibit/soviet.archive.html.
This online exhibit of Soviet-era history is produced by the
Library of Congress. It includes extensive explanations, images
of original documents, and a guided tour.

INDEX

OTHER TITLES FROM LERNER AND A&E®:

Ariel Sharon
Arnold Schwarzenegger
Arthur Ashe
The Beatles
Benjamin Franklin
Bill Gates
Bruce Lee
Carl Sagan
Chief Crazy Horse
Christopher Reeve
Colin Powell
Daring Pirate Women
Edgar Allan Poe
Eleanor Roosevelt
Fidel Castro
George Lucas
George W. Bush
Gloria Estefan
Hillary Rodham Clinton
Jack London
Jacques Cousteau
Jane Austen
Jesse Owens
Jesse Ventura
Jimi Hendrix
John Glenn
Latin Sensations

Legends of Dracula
Legends of Santa Claus
Louisa May Alcott
Madeleine Albright
Malcolm X
Mark Twain
Maya Angelou
Mohandas Gandhi
Mother Teresa
Nelson Mandela
Oprah Winfrey
Osama bin Laden
Princess Diana
Queen Cleopatra
Queen Elizabeth I
Queen Latifah
Rosie O'Donnell
Saddam Hussein
Saint Joan of Arc
Thurgood Marshall
Tiger Woods
Tony Blair
William Shakespeare
Wilma Rudolph
Women in Space
Women of the Wild West
Yasser Arafat

ABOUT THE AUTHOR

Tom Streissguth lives in Florida and works as a writer and editor. He has written more than twenty-five nonfiction books for young people, including biographies and books on history. His volumes in the BIOGRAPHY® series include *Legends of Dracula, Jesse Owens, Queen Cleopatra,* and *John Glenn.* Tom has also written scripts for television.

PHOTO ACKNOWLEDGMENTS

© Dan Herrick-KPA/KEYSTONE Pictures/ZUMA Press, p. 2; © Laski Diffusion/Getty Images, p. 6; © AP | Wide World Photos, pp. 10, 35, 38, 46, 50, 78, 81, 82, 87, 100, 105; Library of Congress, p. 15; © Novosti/Sovfoto, p. 16; © Bettmann/CORBIS, pp. 20, 55; © Peter Turnley/CORBIS, pp. 22, 56; © R.P.G./CORBIS SYGMA, p. 30; © Dirck Halstead/Time Life Pictures/Getty Images, p. 32; © Reuters/ CORBIS, pp. 36, 62, 64, 73, 77, 88, 93; © TASS/Sovfoto, p. 40; © Sergei Guneyev/Time Life Pictures/Getty Images, p. 42; © David Turnley/CORBIS, p. 45; © Keerle Georges de/CORBIS SYGMA, p. 54; © Konstantin Zavrazhin/Getty Images, pp. 66, 84, 95; © East News/Getty Images, p. 69; © Laski Diffusion/Newsmakers/Getty Images, p. 71; © Andrea Booher/FEMA, p. 91; © Stephen JAFFE/ AFP/Getty Images, p. 98; © Sysoyev Grigory/ITAR-TASS/CORBIS, p. 101. **Cover photos:** Front, © ITAR-TASS/Reuters/CORBIS. Back, © Panov Alexei/ITAR-TASS/CORBIS.

WEBSITES